THE REVOLT OF DEMOCRACY
(1913)
BY
ALFRED RUSSEL WALLACE

British Library Cataloguing-in-Publication Data
A catalogue record for this book is available from the
British Library

Alfred Russel Wallace

Alfred Russel Wallace was born on 8th January 1823 in the village of Llanbadoc, in Monmouthshire, Wales.

At the age of five, Wallace's family moved to Hertford where he later enrolled at Hertford Grammar School. He was educated there until financial difficulties forced his family to withdraw him in 1836. He then boarded with his older brother John before becoming an apprentice to his eldest brother, William, a surveyor. He worked for William for six years until the business declined due to difficult economic conditions.

After a brief period of unemployment, he was hired as a master at the Collegiate School in Leicester to teach drawing, map-making, and surveying. During this time he met the entomologist Henry Bates who inspired Wallace to begin collecting insects. He and bates continued exchanging letters after Wallace left teaching to pursue his surveying career. They corresponded on prominent works of the time such as Charles Darwin's *The Voyage of the Beagle* (1839) and Robert Chamber's *Vestiges of the Natural History of Creation* (1844).

Wallace was inspired by the travelling naturalists of the day and decided to begin his exploration career collecting specimens in the Amazon rainforest. He explored the Rio

Negra for four years, making notes on the peoples and languages he encountered as well as the geography, flora, and fauna. On his return voyage his ship, Helen, caught fire and he and the crew were stranded for ten days before being picked up by the Jordeson, a brig travelling from Cuba to London. All of his specimens aboard Helen had been lost.

After a brief stay in England he embarked on a journey to the Malay Archipelago (now Singapore, Malaysia, and Indonesia). During this eight year period he collected more than 126,000 specimens, several thousand of which represented new species to science. While travelling, Wallace refined his thoughts about evolution and in 1858 he outlined his theory of natural selection in an article he sent to Charles Darwin. This was published in the same year along with Darwin's own theory. Wallace eventually published an account of his travels *The Malay Archipelago* in 1869, and it became one of the most popular books of scientific exploration in the 19th century.

Upon his return to England, in 1862, Wallace became a staunch defender of Darwin's landmark work *On the Origin of Species* (1859). He wrote responses to those critical of the theory of natural selection, including 'Remarks on the Rev. S. Haughton's Paper on the Bee's Cell, And on the Origin of Species' (1863) and 'Creation by Law' (1867). The former of these was particularly pleasing to Darwin. Wallace also published important papers such as 'The Origin of Human

Races and the Antiquity of Man Deduced from the Theory of 'Natural Selection" (1864) and books, including the much cited *Darwinism* (1889).

Wallace made a huge contribution to the natural sciences and he will continue to be remembered as one of the key figures in the development of evolutionary theory.

Wallace died on 7th November 1913 at the age of 90. He is buried in a small cemetery at Broadstone, Dorset, England.

THE REVOLT OF DEMOCRACY
(1913)

CHAPTER I. INTRODUCTORY

As President of the Land Nationalisation Society for thirty years, I have given much attention to the various inquiries by Royal Commissions, by Parliamentary Committees, or by private philanthropists, into Irish evictions and Highland clearances, sweating, unemployment, low wages, unhealthy trades, bad and overcrowded dwellings, and the depopulation of the rural districts. These inquiries have succeeded each other in a melancholy procession during the last sixty years; they have made known the almost incredible conditions of life of great numbers of our workers; and they have suggested more or less ineffective remedies, but their proposals have been followed by even less effective legislation when any palliative has been attempted.

During the whole of the nineteenth century there was a continuous advance in the application of scientific discovery to the arts, and especially in the invention and application of labour-saving machinery; and our wealth has increased to an equally marvellous extent. Various estimates which have been made of the increase in our wealth-producing power show that, roughly speaking, the use of mechanical power has increased more than a hundredfold during the century; yet the result has been to create a limited upper class, living in unexampled luxury, while about one-fourth of our whole population exists in a state of fluctuating penury, often sinking below what has been termed "the margin of poverty." Of these, many thousands are annually drawn into the gulf of absolute destitution, dying either from direct starvation, or from diseases produced by their employment, and rendered fatal by want of the necessaries and comforts of a healthy existence.

But during this long period, while wealth and want were alike increasing side by side, public opinion was not sufficiently educated to permit of any effectual remedy being applied for the extirpation of this terrible social disease. The workers themselves had not visualised its fundamental causes--land monopoly and the competitive system of industry, giving rise to an ever-increasing private capitalism which, to a very large extent, controlled the legislature. This rapid growth of wealth through the increase of the various kinds of manufacturing industry led to a still greater increase of middlemen engaged in the distribution of its products, from wealthy merchants, through various grades of tradesmen and petty shopkeepers who supplied the daily wants of the whole community. To these must be added the innumerable parasites of the ever-increasing wealthy classes; the builders of their mansions and their factories; the makers of their furniture and clothing, of their costly ornaments and their children's toys; the vast body of their immediate dependents, from their managers, their agents, commercial travellers and clerks, through various grades of domestic servants, grooms and game-keepers, butlers and housekeepers, down to stable-boys and kitchen-maids, all deriving their means of existence from the wealth daily produced in mines, factories and workshops. This was apparently due primarily, if not exclusively, to the capitalists themselves as the employers of labour, without whose agency and supervision it was believed that all productive labour would cease, bringing ruin and starvation to the whole population. Thus, a vast mass of public opinion was created, all in favour of the capitalists as the employers of labour and the true source of the creation of wealth.

To those who lived in the midst of this vast industrial system, or were a part of it, it seemed natural and inevitable that there should be rich and poor; and this belief was enforced on the one hand by the clergy, and on the other by the political economists, so that religion and science agreed in upholding the competitive and capitalistic system of society as being the only rational and possible one. Hence, till quite recently, it was believed that the abolition of poverty was entirely outside the true sphere of governmental action. It was, in fact, openly declared and believed that poverty was due to economic causes over which governments had no power; that wages were kept down by the "iron law" of supply and demand; and that any attempts to find a remedy by Acts of Parliament only aggravated the disease. This was the doctrine held, even by such great men as W. E. Gladstone and Sir William Harcourt, together with the dogma that it was a government's duty to buy in the cheapest market, in order to protect the taxpayer. It was the doctrine also which converted the misnamed "guardians" of the poor into guardians of the ratepayers' interests, and led to that rigid and unsympathetic treatment of the very poor which made the workhouse more dreaded than the jail, and which to this very day leads many of the most destitute to die of lingering starvation, or to commit suicide, rather than apply for relief or enter the gloomy portals of the workhouse.

CHAPTER II. THE DAWN OF A NEW ERA

It was, I believe, Sir Henry Campbell-Bannerman, when he became Prime Minister in 1905, who changed this attitude of negation of all his predecessors. He boldly declared in numerous speeches, both in and out of Parliament, that he held it to be the duty of a government to deal with the great problems of unemployment and poverty, and especially to attack the increasingly injurious land-monopoly, and so to legislate as to make our native soil ever more and more "a treasure-house for the poor rather than a mere pleasure-house for the rich." And as an earnest of his determination to carry out these views, he brought into his Ministry John Burns and David Lloyd George, the former for his knowledge of the conditions and aspirations of skilled labour, and his administrative experience both in the County Council and in Parliament, and the latter for his energy as an advanced thinker, his powers of public speaking, and his enthusiasm for social reform.

When Mr. Asquith became Prime Minister in 1908, he made Mr. Lloyd George his successor as Chancellor of the Exchequer, and never was the wisdom of an appointment more fully justified. The new Chancellor, in the memorable Budget thrown out by the House of Lords, made provision not only for our ever-increasing Navy, but also for Old-Age

Pensions and for far-reaching measures calculated to benefit the working classes.

It is, in my opinion, largely due to this attitude of Liberal Governments, without adequate remedial legislation, during the last seven years, with a corresponding change in public opinion, that has led to the recent effort of the workers to bring about better conditions by means of combined strikes. The three great strikes in rapid succession, of the Railway and other transport Unions, of the Miners, and of the London Dock Labourers, must have brought home to the middle and upper classes and to the Government how completely they are all dependent on the often despised working classes, not only for every comfort and luxury which they enjoy, for the means of rapid locomotion and of carrying on their respective businesses and pleasures, but also for obtaining the daily food essential for life itself. The experience now gained shows us that when the organisation of the trade unions is rendered more complete, and the accumulated funds of a dozen or twenty years are devoted to this one purpose, the bulk of the inhabitants of London, or of any other of our great cities, could be made to suffer a degree of famine comparable with that of Paris when besieged by the German army in 1870.

It is to be hoped that such a disaster will not happen, but it can only be prevented by much more effective action than has yet been taken to improve the social status of the great body of industrial and other workers, and to abolish completely the conditions which compel a large proportion of those workers to exist on or below the margin of poverty, often culminating in actual death from want of the bare necessaries of existence.

CHAPTER III. THE LESSON OF THE STRIKES

The serious position which these successive strikes have brought about has led to much discussion in the newspapers and other periodicals, in which a number of well-known literary men have taken part, and, what is much more important, in which several of the most able and intelligent of the workers themselves have clearly stated their determination to obtain certain fundamental reforms. Month by month it has become more clear and certain that what has been termed "The Labour Unrest" will certainly continue with ever-increasing determination and effective power till some such reforms as they demand are conceded by the Government.

A careful study of the more important of these various pronouncements shows us that two things stand out clearly, as to which there is almost universal agreement. These are, first, that the condition of the workers as a whole is absolutely unbearable, is a disgrace to civilisation, and fully justifies the most extreme demands of the workers; and, secondly, that among the whole of the writers--whether statesmen or thinkers, capitalists or workmen--there is not one who has proposed any definite and workable plan by which the desired change of conditions will be brought about. Yet one such plan was carefully worked out more than twenty years ago, and though the book had a considerable sale and a cheap edition of it was issued, not the slightest effect was produced on public opinion or on the Government.* The time had not yet come for such radical reforms to be seriously considered. But conditions have changed, and some definite action is now imperatively demanded if this "unrest" is to cease, and if the reasonable claims of the workers are to be satisfied. Let us see, then, what these claims are, and why none of the various palliatives hinted at by a few of those who have taken part in the discussion can do any real good, while they will certainly not satisfy the workers or allay their quite justifiable "unrest."

CHAPTER IV. WHAT THE WORKERS CLAIM AND MUST HAVE

The workers' claim is put forward by Mr. Vernon Hartshorn in the following clear and terse statement: "What is that demand? It is, that the community shall guarantee to the men and women who perform services essential to the existence or happiness of the community, a reasonably comfortable and civilised livelihood--a decent *minimum* of food and clothing, leisure and recreation, and houses fit for human beings." Then he proceeds to ask: "How do the workers propose that the community shall give them that guarantee? By the establishment of a legally guaranteed eight-hours day. By the establishment of a national housing standard at a rent within the reach of the workers. And also by the power of the trade unions to check the exploitation of Labour by competitive methods which tend to force down the average standard of living among the working classes."

Then, after a reference to the recent claim of the doctors to what *they* consider a living wage under the National Insurance Act, and also to the many luxuries of the rich which the workers do *not* want, he again states the workers' claim thus: "It is not an extravagant demand. It is just the plain blunt demand that might be expected from British working-men . . . It is a demand by those who, either by hand

16

or brain, make the wealth of the nation, that the first charge upon that wealth shall be the maintenance of themselves in reasonable comfort."

Then he concludes with this important declaration of policy:--

"Democracy must be its own emancipator. But institutions like the Church, Parliament, and the Press, and even the rich, have to make up their minds as to what shall be their attitude toward it. They must decide for themselves whether the demand of the workers for a fairer share of the good things of life is just or unjust. The working classes have already made up their minds. They are convinced that their demand is just, and with a highly intelligent, vigorous working class, stung by a sense of injustice, the future of this country will be full of danger. The stupid attitude of hostility or superior patronage which has been adopted towards the working classes in the past by powerful elements in society has helped to generate the present revolutionary upheaval . . . The worker does not want charity to redress the balance. He knows that charity robs him of his manhood. He feels that he is entitled to a man's share of the wealth he has produced, and he wants it assured to him, not as a charity, but as a citizen's right."

Then, after describing how neither Parliament nor the present Government can or will secure this for him, and that their methods of "conciliation" or "arbitration" are useless or inadequate, he concludes:

"There is only one way to industrial peace. There is only one way to stave off a class war which may shake civilisation to its foundations.

It is by a full and frank acknowledgement by society that the claim of the worker to a sufficiency of food and clothing and a fuller life is just, and that it must be made the first charge upon the wealth produced . . . It is the present order of society which is upon its trial. Can it do justice to the worker? If it can, and if it does, then it will have justified its existence. But if it cannot, then its ultimate doom is sealed."

Quotations from other Labour leaders could be made to the same effect, showing that the workers now *know* their rights and are determined to obtain them. But they do *not* see exactly how that is to be done, and it is for their friends and well-wishers to assist them in finding out a way.

A few useful indications of how we must approach the problem may be quoted.

Mr. Seebohm Rowntree, one of the best and most sympathetic employers of labour in the country, tells us that--"The capitalists should entirely shake off the idea that wage-earners are inferior beings to themselves, and should learn to regard them as valued and necessary partners in the great work of wealth-production--partners with whose accredited representatives they may honourably discuss the proportions in which the wealth jointly produced should be divided." He also sees clearly, and declares that--"The poverty at one end of the social scale will not be removed except by encroaching heavily upon the great riches at the other end." But this, apparently, is the last thing capitalist employers want or will submit to.

Mr. Frederic Harrison urges that labour cannot be in a settled and healthy state "till seven hours is made the normal standard of a day's labour," and that--"a fixed living wage is merely the irreducible part of the remuneration, the rest being proportioned to the profits on the work done." And he concludes his most interesting and suggestive article with the dictum that--"The unrest is come to stay, and will not be ended by petty devices."

Mr. Sidney Low tells us that there are many young men among the workers who read Carlyle and Ruskin, and believe that if our society were rightly organised the life of cultivated leisure would not be the privilege of the Few, but the possession of the Many. Mr. Geoffrey Drage confirms this statement, and declares that--"the worker sees that the time for cries is past, the time for action is come."

But he, too, like all the others, gives no clue as to how the great change is to be brought about, not sporadically here and there, but universally--not by slightly improving the condition of skilled labour only, but by such means as will immediately begin to act upon the lowest stratum of the social fabric, and in a measurable space of time abolish want, culminating in actual starvation, in this land of ever-increasing wealth, and ever more and more extravagant luxury.

Before laying before my readers what I conceive to be, at the present juncture, the best and, indeed, the *only* mode of successfully attacking this great and pressing problem, I will give the statement of Mr. Anderson, the Chairman of the Conference of the Independent Labour Party, in the autumn of 1912. In reply to a Press representative, he said: "The whole upheaval is a revolt against poverty; against, that is, Social Injustice; and it involves the Right to Live . . . Strikes are disintegrating . . . they are no real and permanent remedy. We have to find the solution in some new basis for industrial reform, and my view is, that if reform is to do any good *it must contain in itself the germ of a better social organisation.* Palliatives are no cure."

And then, when he was urged to say, "What do you actually propose?" his reply was: "We are determined that *destitution must be stamped out;* and our remedy resolves itself into this: *A national minimum of Wages, Housing, Leisure, and Education. That is Labour's battle-cry for the future."*

CHAPTER V. A GOVERNMENT'S DUTY

Now, in all the foregoing views of the leaders and the friends of Labour, there is a very close agreement as to the present position of the whole body of workers, and as to the nature and amount of the reforms they insist upon, without which they will not be satisfied, and will not cease from agitation, culminating in more extensive and more determined and better-organised strikes. This will be the only method left open to them if their admittedly moderate and just claims are not fully and honestly recognised by the party in power, and at once translated into adequate *direct action.*

It is a very strange thing to me, and must be so to many others, that in this most wealthy country a powerful Government, long pledged to social reform, *cannot* or *will not* take any immediate and direct steps to abolish the pitiable extremes of destitution which are ever present in all its great cities, its towns, and even its villages! The old, complex and harsh machinery of its Poor Laws has become less and less efficient. Enormous sums spent in various forms of charity do not prevent starvation, do not appear to diminish it. The cause of this almost universal apathy is the very persistence of destitution and its obscurity. The various forms of charity are more conspicuous and more obtrusive, so that most people are quite unable to realise that starvation is still rampant to a most terrible and most disgraceful extent all over our land.

In 1898 I published in my volume on *The Wonderful Century* an appendix on "The Remedy for Want in the Midst of Wealth," but, thinking that the general scheme I proposed was too advanced for immediate adoption, I also gave a plan, headed "How to Stop Starvation," which began with these words: "But till some such method is demanded by public opinion, and its adoption forced upon our legislators, the horrible scandal and crime of men, women, and little children, by thousands and millions, living in the most wretched want, dying of actual starvation, or driven to suicide by the dread of it, *must be stopped!*"

The Chairman of the Independent Labour Party now also declares that "Destitution must be stamped out."

Since the above passage was written nothing effective has been done, the horrors of our slums are as bad as ever, our cumbrous and unsympathetic systems of poor relief are utter failures. I, therefore, again submit my simple and practical suggestion, which is as much needed to-day as it was then. It is as follows:

"The only certain way to abolish starvation, not when it is too late, but in its very earliest stages, is *free bread*. I imagine the outcry against this: 'Fraud! Loafing! Pauperisation!' etc., etc. Perhaps so; perhaps not. But even if it *must* be so, better give bread to a hundred loafers than refuse it to a hundred who are starving. *All* who want it, *all* who have not money enough to buy wholesome food and other necessaries, must be able to get this bread with the minimum of trouble. There must be no *tests* like those for Poor Law relief. A decent home, with good furniture and good clothes, must be no bar; neither must the possession of money if that money is needed for rent, for coals, or for other absolute necessaries of life. The bread must be given to *prevent* injurious destitution, not merely to alleviate it. The bread is *not* to be charity, *not* poor relief, but a rightful claim upon society for its neglect to organise itself so that *all*, without exception, who have worked, and are willing to work, or are unable to work, may at the very least have food to support life.

"Now for the mode of obtaining this bread. All local authorities shall be required to prepare bread-tickets duly stamped and numbered with coupons to be detached, each representing a 2-lb. or 4-lb. loaf. These tickets to be issued in suitable quantities to every policeman, to all the clergy of every denomination, and to all medical men. Any person in want of food, by applying to any of these distributors is to be given a coupon for one loaf, *without any question whatever.*

"If the person wants more than one loaf, or wishes to have one or more such loaves for a week, a name and address must be given. The distributor, or some deputy, will then pay a visit during the day, ascertain the bare facts, give a suitable number of tickets, and, as in cases of sickness or of young children, obtain such other relief as may be needed."

The cost of dealing with this widespread destitution should be borne by the National Exchequer, both because it is due to deep-seated causes in our social economy, and also because its distribution is very unequal, so that the cost would be heaviest in the poorer and lightest in the richer areas. It must, however, be treated as essentially of a temporary nature, only needed till the fundamental causes of poverty are properly dealt with by some such method as that to be explained later on, when any such expedient will become a thing of the past.

When we consider that during the last fourteen years our national expenditure has increased by about 80,000,000, and that it has now reached the vast amount of 185,000,000, it is almost incredible that we should have made no serious attempt to discover the causes and apply the remedy to this terrible social canker in our civilisation. Now, however, that the Labour Party insists upon an immediate remedy being applied, and also claims for the sufferers and for the whole body of workers full social equality with all other citizens--a claim recognised by many of our best and greatest writers to be a just one--perennial starvation of our very poor must no longer be ignored, and our Government must grapple with it without further delay.

Government and Its Employees

We will now proceed to consider how the Government can itself lead the way towards that new organisation of society which will afford a permanent remedy for labour unrest, and satisfy the just demands of some considerable portion of the workers of our country.

The Prime Minister has quite recently declared his invincible objection to fixing even a minimum wage by Act of Parliament, but no positive objection has been made to raising the wages of all Government employees above such a minimum. This has been asked for again and again by the workers themselves, as well as by their representatives in Parliament, but has only been acted upon partially, and any proposal for giving higher wages than are paid by private capitalists has been objected to for various reasons. It is said to be unfair to thus compete with private enterprise; that more men at present wages can always be had than are required; and other reasons of the usual type of the old school of economists. These objections are also upheld for political reasons, since the large number of capitalists and wealthy employers of labour in the House of Commons would violently oppose any such unprecedented expenditure, and endanger the very existence of the Government.

But all these objections may now, perhaps, be much weakened, or even disregarded, in view of the recent strikes and the future possibilities they suggest. The workers are now steadily becoming better organised and more conscious of their own power at the polls, and they will no longer support a Government which confesses itself impotent to lift them out of the terrible quagmire of misery and degradation into which the present *economic system* is steadily forcing them. The time for conferences and discussions and for petty alleviations which are wholly useless is gone by. What the workers now demand is that the Government shall begin to act so far as it possesses the power to act; that it must raise the wages, provide decent houses, establish shorter hours of work, give suitable holidays, and establish liberal retiring pensions, *for every one of its own employees.*

It is true that something has been done in this direction, but many Government workers are still said to be as badly off as under the lower class of private capitalists. Whether or not this is due to the old idea that the taxpayers *must* be protected though the children of the workers suffer want, I do not know; but unless this economy in the wrong place is changed, and the very reverse principle acted upon, the present Government will bring upon itself the united opposition of the workers.

What then must our rulers do in the present crisis? To use the forcible expression of the late W. T. Stead, what we insist upon now is, *that we declare war against every form of want, poverty, and industrial discontent, and that the Government must lead the way and set the pace.* It must do this because it is the greatest employer of labour in the kingdom: its Civil Service alone--the receivers of annual salaries instead of weekly wages--comprising 136,000 persons; and because it has the power of influencing all other employers of labour through the force of its example, as well as by the action of economic laws.

In order to give confidence to the Labour Party, a proclamation should be at once issued establishing for the entire Government Service a liberal scale of wages, based upon the inquiries of Mr. C. Booth, Mr. S. Rowntree and others, so that adult workers shall receive at next pay-day an ample "living wage," to be increased each year by (say) 2s. a week till it reaches the estimate of these disinterested and capable inquirers. Let it be declared also that, except for *gross bad conduct,* no man shall be dismissed [from] the public service till he reaches the age when he will receive a liberal retiring pension.

As the avowed object *must be* to make Government employment at once an honour and an advantage, and also that it may serve as a model for all other employers of labour, everything must be done to promote the health and contentment of the whole body of public workers. In order to give effect to this declared purpose, a considerable proportion of them should be gradually trained in some alternative employment, especially in those that give healthy outdoor occupation, such as the various building trades, and, pre-eminently, in some kind of agricultural work. It will thus be rendered possible, whenever we cease to expend so many millions annually on purely destructive ships and weapons, that the surplus men engaged in our dockyards and various factories of war-material need not be discharged and create a new army of the unemployed, but be gradually drafted into an army of true *wealth-producers*.

Another important feature of this new departure in the organisation of the extended Civil Service would be the gradual removal of all factories and workshops from towns and cities into the open and healthy country, where large areas of land can be obtained sufficient to produce most of the food and clothing for its inhabitants. Large estates of several thousand acres are constantly in the market, and are often sold at from £10 to £20 an acre. An additional means of obtaining such estates would be a short Act giving the Government power to take death-duties and land-taxes in land at the taxation value whenever it is suitable for the purpose. Of course, acting on the general principle of making its own employees and labourers the best and most contented of all the working classes, the Government must at once make arrangements for giving up its contract work, especially in the clothing and provision departments, replacing it by farms and factories of its own.

CHAPTER VI. POPULAR OBJECTIONS, AND REPLIES TO THEM

The scheme of improved Government employment now briefly explained will, of course, give rise to a host of objections of various degrees of futility, but I know of none of the least real weight. The first of these objections will, of course, be the great expense; and that it will necessitate more taxes, which will ruin those who only just manage to live now. To this I reply, that the cost to the poor need really be almost *nothing*; first, because every pound paid extra in wages is a pound more expended in food, clothing, furniture, houses, and other necessaries of life. It will, therefore, benefit the makers, growers and retailers of those commodities by the increase of their trade, and it is a maxim of political economy that the home trade is the best trade for the prosperity of a country. In the second place, even with our present system of taxation the workers will largely benefit, because, though they will secure almost all the immediate good results of the expenditure, they will pay less than half the increased taxation.

But, fortunately, we have a Chancellor of the Exchequer who will know how to raise the money required for the salvation of the destitute from the excessive and harmful accumulations of the very rich. The lower and middle classes, therefore, will ultimately pay either nothing at all or a very small fraction of the amount required for the increased wages, while they are the classes which will most largely benefit by the general prosperity caused by its expenditure. It must surely be better for the country to preserve the very poor in health and strength, and to give them the training which will enable them to do productive work as soon as we provide it for them, than to allow them to die and want, and its resulting diseases, as we do now. It is simply irrational to say, as many do, that these people are constitutionally unable to support themselves. They belong to the very same class as those who, both here and in the Colonies, and throughout the whole civilised world, not only *do* support themselves, but, in addition, support everybody else, and at the same time produce *all the luxuries and costly amusements of the wealthy.* It is clear, therefore, that it is not the fault of the poor that so many of them are compulsorily idle or starving, but of the Government which proclaims itself unable to give them productive work. There cannot possibly be such a difference in nature between the same class when employed and when unemployed.

Another objection, a little less obviously irrational, is, that if the Government itself were to provide all its Army and Navy clothing and other necessary stores, weapons, etc., some of the former contractors will be ruined. But they will only suffer if they have hitherto sweated their workers, and you cannot abolish sweating without some temporary suffering to the sweaters. But even such employers will get compensation. The high wages paid for all Government work will be almost wholly spent in the neighbourhood of the public factories and offices, and benefit everybody by the increase of trade. A further benefit will accrue through the increased expenditure of the many thousands of Custom House, Excise, Post Office, and other employees, whose higher wages and salaries would be immediately distributed among the various producers and retailers of the necessaries and comforts of life--that is, among those constituting what we term generally "the middle classes," who may be said to constitute the very backbone of the country.

CHAPTER VII. THE PROBLEM OF WAGES

High Wages Are Good for Everybody

If we look at the great problem of wages, as affecting the entire life and well-being of about three-fourths of the whole population, and try and divest ourselves of our ideas of what wages a particular kind of worker is worth, without any regard to the material and mental well-being of his wife and children, we shall be forced to the conclusion that nothing is so *hurtful* to the community at large, especially to the middle classes, as for the wages or earnings of all kinds of workers to be low; and nothing is so *beneficial* as for them to be high.

A Government cannot benefit its people at large more surely than by establishing a very high *minimum wage* for really necessary or useful work. Every thinker agrees (as they did at the Industrial Remuneration Conference held twenty-five years ago) that our aim and object should be "*to cause wealth to be more equally distributed.*" Yet, during the whole period that has elapsed since that Conference was held, successive Governments have acted as if their object was the *very reverse;* with the natural result of increasing the number both of millionaires at one end of the scale, and of the excessively poor and destitute at the other. And they actually claim this as a merit; for their supporters always refer to the increase of great fortunes made mostly by foreign trade as a proof of general prosperity, and have always resisted giving their own employees more than a bare competition wage, on the ground that it was their chief duty to save the pockets of the taxpayers!

The Just Basis of Taxation

Till quite recently our various Governments, whatever party has been in power, have claimed it as a merit that they have distributed taxation as equally as possible over the whole community, on the ground that the very poorest ought to contribute something towards the Government of which they are said to receive the benefits of law and order at home, and protection from invasion by foreign armies. We are now seeing the results of this policy in labour unrest, chronic strikes, and terrible destitution. The beginning of a juster and wiser policy has been made in the differential taxation of very large incomes, but only a very small beginning. Justice and humanity alike should lead us to see that those who, by their hard and life-long toil, have created and still create the whole of the national wealth, should not be taxed on the very small portion of that wealth which they have been allowed to retain--a bare sufficiency to support life. Justice and public policy alike demand that every penny of taxation should be taken from the superfluously wealthy at or near the other end of the scale. Thus, and thus only, could we cause the present insufficient *minimum* wage to rise, first above the bare subsistence rate, and then by a steady increase to an amount sufficient to procure for all our workers the essentials for a full and enjoyable existence. Thus, and thus only, can we solve the crucial problem of our day, that of the long expected and perfectly justifiable revolt of the workers, euphemistically termed the "Labour Unrest."

The Class-Prejudice Against High Wages

Perhaps more difficult to overcome than the supposed economical dangers of high wages is the class-prejudice. This is really due to differences of education, of forms of speech and of manners, rather than to any real difference either in physical or mental powers. As human beings the workers with their hands, commonly called the "working class," know themselves to be fully equal to those who look down upon them as inferiors; and they are beginning to resent this claim to superiority. They know, too, that their work is really more important than that of many professional men, such as lawyers and the mass of Government officials, and that the scale of remuneration of the two classes should be more nearly alike. The idea that the work of a carpenter or engineer, of a bricklayer or of a ploughman is intrinsically *worth* less than that of a Member of Parliament, an officer in the Army, or the owner of a cotton-mill they no longer accept. They have read history, and they know that these class-ideas are derived from feudal times, when all manual labour was done by serfs, or by peasants only one degree higher in the scale. They see many of their own class becoming rich, and then being received as equals by those who term themselves "Society"; and they see, too, that these upstarts, as they are sometimes termed, are often not even the best examples of their own class.

It is this widespread belief in there being a "lower class" among us--hewers of wood and drawers of water--whose *intrinsic worth* as human beings is measured by the small wages they receive, that causes the proposal to raise their earnings to what we now term "a living wage" to be widely resented, as if it were something dangerous, unnecessary, or even immoral.

Most liberal thinkers now agree that wages *ought* to be much higher than they are; but unless they rise automatically in obedience to some mysterious economic law, not even the most advanced Government in the most advanced country in the world has yet dared to make the attempt to improve the condition of its vast army of employees by raising them, on principle, well above "the margin of poverty." So great and so widespread is this objection that there are, perhaps, not more than two or three members of our present Government who would welcome with any approach to enthusiasm such a proposal as I have outlined here. When it was recently stated that certain classes of men in the Navy were to receive an increase of pay it was at first denied, as if it were too extravagant to be thought of by an economical Liberal Government.

It is, however, certain that we have now reached a point in our political history which will necessitate much more direct and radical measures than have yet been taken to ensure the immediate abolition of that disgrace of our civilisation--starvation, and suicide from dread of starvation.

It is for this reason that I have now placed before the public the simplest and most direct method of doing this, without any *special* legislation; and I most earnestly urge the Labour Party, as well as advanced thinkers of all parties in Parliament, to use their influence with the present Government to give it effect.

The wages of the lower classes of Government clerks, etc., are, I believe, being frequently modified by the various heads of departments without any special sanction from Parliament; and as I have now shown how every step of the process of more equal wealth-distribution by a steady rise of wages will injure few or none, but will in various ways benefit us all, there can be no sufficiently serious objection to its being immediately begun.

I would also with equal earnestness urge upon the Government *itself* to press forward this matter--the abolition of destitution--without a single day's further delay. Every day sees numerous deaths by starvation at our very doors. Yet these have come to be looked upon as due to "natural causes," implying that it is quite a natural and inevitable thing that, in this super-wealthy country, thousands of men, women, and children should be continually starving! Were not the position so terribly, so disgracefully pathetic, it would be ludicrous. It reminds one of David Copperfield's arrival at his aunt's house at Dover in a dreadfully dilapidated condition after a six days' walk from London, having slept every night in the fields. Mr. Dick was called to hear his story; and on being asked by Miss Betsy Trotwood what she should do with him, looked him all over very carefully, and said without hesitation: "If I were you, I should wash him." On which Miss Betsy ordered a hot bath to be got ready, declaring that Mr. Dick sets us all right!

But the most advanced and Liberal Government we have ever had, has for the last seven years looked on tens of thousands of destitute humanity far worse off than was David Copperfield, without arriving at the practical wisdom of *first* feeding and clothing them, and *afterwards* inquiring and discussing how to prevent them from getting into the same trouble again. I, therefore, take the place of poor Mr. Dick as an adviser, and venture to assure them that the problem is *not* really insoluble, and that the common idea, that the pitiable condition of the starving population is *"their own fault,"* is *not* the correct diagnosis of this social disease.

Popular Errors as to the Effects of High Wages on Prices

One of the most common objections to a general increase of wages, and one of the most difficult to reply to, is, that it would inevitably lead to a general rise of prices, equal to, and sometimes greater than, the increase of wages. The reason why it is difficult to reply to this supposed fact is because the retail prices of the necessaries of life depend upon a variety of causes, of which a rise or fall in the wages of those who produce them is sometimes an important and at other times a very unimportant item; and also because, as a matter of fact, wages and prices have, sometimes, risen or fallen together as if they were directly connected.

This whole question of the well-being of the wage-receiving classes is often obscured by considering wages alone, or hours of working, or prices of food, which may all vary in different degrees, and be due to quite different causes. The result thus reached is often largely modified by an increase of rents, of rates, or in the price of such a necessary as coals, while a still further complication is introduced by local causes, such as the time, labour, or cost of reaching his place of work, which may seriously reduce a workman's net earnings, as well as his hours of actual labour. Personal observation during the last fifty years leads me to conclude that, amid constant fluctuations in wages and in food prices, and constant rise in the rental of houses and of land, the average wage-earner has continued to live in much the same low condition as regards the necessaries and comforts of life.

But during this whole period there has been a continuous increase in the numbers of the very poor, the destitute, and the actually starving; serving as a balance to a similar increase in the numbers of those who live in great or superfluous luxury. Let us then endeavour to see how this long-continued process and baneful result can be changed in the future.

CHAPTER VIII. SELF-SUPPORTING WORK
THE REMEDY FOR UNEMPLOYMENT

As a matter of public policy, no less than of common humanity, it is essential that all Government and municipal employees, including labourers of all kinds, be paid a full and sufficient living wage as a *minimum,* rising to at least the highest trades union wages at the time. To prevent any lowering of the latter, by increase of population, fluctuations in trade, new labour-saving machinery and other causes of unemployment, it is equally essential that those who have hitherto been discharged when no longer wanted should be provided with self-supporting work.

This can best be done in connection with the re-occupation of the land, which is now seen to be of vital importance by most social reformers. No more blind and disastrous policy has ever been pursued by a civilised community than that of our wealthy and money-making classes, who have during half-a-century, in pursuit of wealth, discouraged the cultivation of land, and forced the inhabitants of our once numerous self-supporting villages, and especially our half-starved agricultural labourers, into the cities and towns, to be exploited by manufacturers and landlords. The result to-day is a vast mass of unemployed, keeping down wages to the starving point, together with an infant mortality that is a disgrace to a civilised community.

Having thus destroyed the old rural populations which were for centuries the pride and strength of Britain, it now becomes the duty of the Government to build up a new and a better form of rural society to replace it. To do this we require far stronger measures than the miserable red-tapism of our Small Holdings Acts, which are ludicrously ineffective and even harmful. We have examples in Denmark, in Italy, and even in Ireland, of admirable results of co-operative cultivation, where extensive areas of land are dealt with, and either private or municipal associations help on the work.

For this purpose a large portion of the agricultural land of England, which has been so misused by its owners, must be acquired by the Government in trust for the nation. This can be best done by a further increase of the death duties and land taxes; to be paid in land itself instead of in money: while, wherever there are no direct heirs who may have a sentimental affection for their ancestral home, large landed estates of suitable character and position should be purchased at the official valuation and utilised at once either by the State, the municipality, trade unions, or co-operative societies, to establish self-supporting colonies, on the plan first clearly described by Mr. Herbert V. Mills in his *Poverty and the State*, and further developed by myself in the second volume of my *Studies, Scientific and Social.*

The great essentials in starting such methods of dealing with the problems of poverty and unemployment are *liberality* and *sympathy*. Ample funds should be provided for supporting each colony for the first two or three years; the land should be rent-free for at least the same period; and the greatest amount of liberty should be given to all the workers compatible with the success of the experiments. No expense can be too great to establish a system of land re-occupation which will abolish poverty; and just as certainly as a continuous rise in wages will repay its cost in the general well-being of the lower and middle classes, so, with equal certainty, will the still greater expenditure necessary for the productive re-occupation of our uncultivated or half-cultivated soil complete the regeneration, the power, and the safety of the British nation.

Everyone interested in the subject here discussed should read *Our National Food Supply*, by James Lumsden: perhaps the most original, suggestive, and vitally important work on the subject that has yet appeared.

One of the injurious results of our competitive system, having its roots, however, in the valuable "guilds" of a past epoch, is the almost universal restriction of our workers to one kind of labour only. The result is a dreadful monotony in almost all kinds of work, the extreme unhealthiness of many, and a much larger amount of unemployment than if each man or woman were regularly trained in two or more occupations. In addition to two of what are commonly called trades, every youth should be trained for one day a week or one week in a month, according to demand for labour, in some of the various operations of farming or gardening. Not only would this improve the general health of the workers, but also add much to the interest and enjoyment of their lives. This is a matter of great national importance, because it would supply in every locality a body of trained workers ready to assist the farmers at all critical periods, and thus save valuable crops from almost total loss during unfavourable seasons. The gain to the whole nation by such a supply of labour, whenever needed, would be enormous, and it would also lead to pleasant social meetings like those of the "bees" in the early years of American colonisation. Such gatherings would combine a holiday with national service, when the whole strength of the population would be put forth to save the national food.

This form of multiple industrial training should be commenced at once in connection with all Government employment; and it should be further developed as a part of our system of education, in the various colonies or villages established for the absorption of the unemployed. Its advantages would be so great both to the workers and to the nation, that the various trade unions may be expected to adopt it; and they should be assisted to do so by ample

Government grants, or by the free provision of the land and buildings required, so long as they were used for this great national service.

CHAPTER IX. THE ECONOMIES OF CO-ORDINATED LABOUR

It may be well here to consider what would be the economic result if the labour of the whole country were completely organised and its various departments co-ordinated, so that production and consumption should be as nearly as possible balanced in the various local communities. This local co-ordination of production and distribution has never, hitherto, been attempted on an adequate scale, yet it is through such co-ordination alone that co-operative labour can produce its most beneficial results, by means of a number of hitherto unknown and apparently almost unsuspected economies, to the enormous gain of the whole community. The more important of these may be briefly enumerated. The first of these great economies would arise from the absence of surplus crops or manufactured goods beyond the ascertained monthly or yearly amount required for the use of the local population. From this approximate balance of production with consumption the proportional cost of each article in labour-power would be calculated, and their several exchange-values or true economic prices be ascertained. The use of a more expensive article when a less costly one would be equally serviceable would then be easily checked, and the great loss incurred by the forced sale of such articles would cease.

Far more important than this, however, would be the entire abolition of every form of advertisement, such as those in our newspapers and placards, in costly shop-windows, in high rents, and in the employment of a whole army of agents and commercial travellers, whose business is to puff and exaggerate the qualities of their respective goods, so as to induce retailers and private purchasers to buy things that are of little or no use to them, and often, as in the case of foods and medicines, positively injurious.

It has been estimated that, on the average, these costly processes of competitive sale lead to the consumer paying about double, and in some cases much more than double, the real cost of production. Here, then, we have an economy which would enable wages to be largely increased, and sometimes even doubled, without adding to the retail price of the various necessaries or comforts of life. But even this would not be the whole of the economy that would follow such a mode of truly co-ordinated production for use and not for profit. It is well known that in all manufactured goods a large economy results from an increased demand, enabling the whole of the machinery to be almost continuously employed at its full power. In addition to this, another economy of the same nature, but perhaps of still greater extent, would arise from there being no such necessity for the manufacture of *new articles* or new patterns or colours every year, as the competition of numerous manufacturers now compels them to seek for. These new things or patterns are often very inferior to the older ones, which the purchaser is assured "are quite gone out now."

As a concomitant of the competitive system, two almost world-wide immoralities are created: one is the universal practice of adulteration and the accompanying false descriptions of things sold; the other is the equally vast system of false weights and measures, which, though of small amount to each purchaser, secures an unfair profit at his expense. Our present competitive social system is, therefore, necessarily immoral, as well as extremely wasteful; yet, strange to say, it is almost universally held to be a necessary and a right system, founded on natural and unchangeable laws of social life. Those who see most clearly its evil results, and trace them to their root causes, monopoly and competition, are almost always condemned as unpractical idealists or dangerous revolutionists.

Another proof of the fundamental error of this system of society which is held to be so good and sacred as to be essentially unalterable is equally conducive. For more than a century this system has been slowly elaborated by a body of able men who are so admired by us, that we term them our "Merchant princes" and our "Captains of industry." Many of them are enormously wealthy and are supposed to be especially qualified as Members of Parliament, and they possess great influence in directing the course of legislation.

Yet this wealth and power were obtained by means of a system of industry which soon became a byword for all that was vile and degrading to the workers who were employed. Everything was arranged so as to get the most profit out of the "hands," as the factory-workers were termed. The mills were unhealthy, the wages low, and the hours of labour long. In the early part of the nineteenth century, children of five or six years old were kept in the mills thirteen or fourteen hours a day, and were often flogged by the overseers to keep them awake; and it needed a long succession of Factory Laws, all bitterly opposed by the employers, to mitigate the evils which till recently existed, and which were only got rid of by the continued efforts of a few determined humanitarians. An army of inspectors had to be appointed to see that these laws were obeyed. Yet even now the net result of our strictly supervised manufacturing system is that whole districts are defaced by dense palls of smoke, and the vegetation is often destroyed by poisonous vapours; that our great cities are disfigured by hideous and filthy slums; that a large proportion of our manufactures are carried on under such conditions as to produce painful disabling or fatal diseases; while the infant mortality in all these areas of wealth-production, of which we are so proud, is about double what it is in other parts of the same towns or cities.

The various facts and considerations now adduced demonstrate that a well-arranged system of co-operative production and co-ordinated distribution, whether carried out by the Government, municipality, or private associations of the workers, which the trade unions themselves might combine to establish, would result in so many economies in various directions as to render it possible in a few years to double, or more than double, the effective wages the workers now receive, but which, under existing conditions, they can only hope to raise by the slow and costly process of recurrent strikes. This sketch of the economics of the problem is now brought before the Labour Party in order that it may have a definite programme to work for, and may be able to enforce its claims upon the Government with all the weight of its combined and determined action.

CHAPTER X. THE EFFECT OF HIGH WAGES UPON FOREIGN TRADE

I have now shown that an increase in the rate of wages does not necessarily raise prices in a proportionate degree, but, on the contrary, that, under conditions not difficult to obtain, such enormous economies both in production and distribution may be effected as to result in a very large balance in favour both of the producer and the consumer. This, however, relates to our home trade only, and it will be said, and has often been said, that as regards our foreign trade the case is quite different. In such goods as minerals, metal-work, and most textile fabrics, wages form a large portion of the cost, and it is argued that a considerable rise will render us quite unable to compete with Germany, France, or America in the chief markets of the world.

Now, it is a remarkable circumstance that the Labour Party and their friends in and out of Parliament seem to be quite unaware of the fallacy of this statement. It is quite true that if wages rose in one industry only, our foreign trade might be injured or even ruined in those special goods. But if, as is here supposed to be the case, there was a general rise of wages in all industries, such as would be caused by bringing about a high "living wage," sufficient at its lowest to keep every workman and his family in health and comfort with a reasonable amount of the enjoyments of life, then our foreign trade in the markets of the world would not in any way be diminished or become less profitable.

This results from the fact admitted by all political economists, that foreign trade is essentially barter, since we send abroad those goods which we produce at the lowest cost proportionately, and import those only which no other country produces at a lower proportionate cost than we do. In this set of transactions, as a whole, the part played by money is merely to enable both parties to keep their accounts and determine what goods it is advantageous to them to export and what to import. Hence money has been defined as the "tool of exchange." If, therefore, our wages bill were doubled by the adoption of a high "minimum wage," that would not make any alteration (or very little) in the *proportionate cost* of the things we export and those we import.

This question is discussed with great care and thoroughness by J. S. Mill, in his great work, *The Principles of Political Economy*; but as the subject is referred to more than once, and for different purposes, it requires very close attention to realise its full importance. It is discussed most fully in his Book III., Chap. XVII., "Of International Trade," where he says: "It is not a difference in the *absolute* cost of production which determines the interchange, but a difference in the comparative cost"; and this is illustrated by an account of many actual cases of our dealings with other countries, in which he shows that--"We may often by trading with foreigners obtain their commodities at a smaller expense of labour and capital than they cost to the foreigners themselves. The bargain is still advantageous to the foreigner, because the commodity which he receives in exchange, though it has cost us less, would have cost him more."

Then, later on, in Chap. XXV. of the same Book, dealing with "Competition of Countries in the same Market" (page 414 of The People's Edition), he says, as a terse summary of the facts and arguments he has set forth: "General low wages never caused any country to undersell its rivals, nor did general high wages ever hinder it from doing so."

I venture to hope that, in future, the speakers among the Labour Party in Parliament will not allow the bugbear of "ruin to our foreign trade" to deter them from claiming their admitted right to a "living wage" throughout the whole country. Such wage must be determined by what is needed to supply an average working-man's family with all the necessaries of life in ample abundance, together with all such modest comforts as are beneficial to health of mind and body. It must be estimated as payment for five or five and a half days of eight hours each at the utmost, any overtime necessitated by the nature of the employment or by exceptional events to be paid at double the normal rates.

I have now shown that a general rise of wages, if

accompanied by the absorption of all the unemployed in duly co-ordinated *productive labour*, so far from raising prices in the open market, will result in so many and such great economies as to allow of a considerable lowering of price of the chief necessaries and comforts of life, and will, therefore, add still further to the well-being of the whole of the workers, whether skilled or unskilled, whether receiving wages from capitalist employers, or working in co-operative and self-supporting village communities.

CHAPTER XI. THE RATIONAL SOLUTION OF THE LABOUR PROBLEM

I have now endeavoured to place before my readers, and especially before the Labour Party, the series of economic fallacies which alone prevent them from claiming and obtaining, for the workers of the whole country, a continuously increasing share of the entire product of their labour.

The chief of these fallacies is, that there is any *necessary* connection between wages and prices, so that the former cannot be raised without the latter increasing also to an equal amount. Of course, in such a fundamentally unjust social system as that in which we live, we cannot abolish *all* the wrongs and evils of low wages, unemployment, and starvation, by a more just and rational system without partial and temporary losses to a few individuals; but by adopting the course here advocated, these losses will be small in amount and quickly remedied. This will be especially the case with our foreign trade, as to which it has been again and again asserted that higher wages will lead to ruin. But, as has been clearly shown in the preceding chapter, no such loss would occur if high wages were universal, such as would result from a general minimum of 30s. or £2 a week for every adult worker in the kingdom, while a large majority would receive much more than this. Even in such an extreme case as this our merchants might continue to export and import the same products in the same quantities as before, and with the same average amount of profit.

Recurring to the statements of Mr. Vernon Hartshorn and Mr. Anderson as to what the workers insist upon as the very lowest living wage, but which it is clear they will *never* obtain by negotiation with their employers, I again urge upon them to concentrate their rapidly increasing influence and voting power upon the Government, compelling it to use the full resources of the National Credit to abolish starvation at once, and simultaneously to organise the vast body of Government employees in such a manner as to be able to absorb into its ranks the whole of the unemployed workers as they arise. These may be looked upon as the waste product of our disorganised and inhuman competitive system, indicating the fermentation and disease ever going on in its lower depths.

The principle of competition--a life and death struggle for bare existence-- has had more than a century's unbroken trial under conditions created by its upholders, *and it has absolutely failed.* The workers, now for the first time, know *why* it is that with ever-increasing production of wealth so many of them still suffer the most terrible extremes of want and of preventable disease. There must, therefore, be no further compromise, no mere talking. To allow the present state of things to continue is a crime against humanity. Any Government that *will* not abolish starvation in this land of superfluous wealth must be driven from power. The forces of Labour, if united in the demand for this one *primary* object, must and will succeed. Then will easily follow the general rise of wages at the cost of our unprecedented individual wealth, and the absorption of the unemployed in self-supporting communities, re-occupying our deserted land, and bringing about a more general and more beneficial prosperity than our country has ever before enjoyed.

This must be the great and noble work of our statesmen of to-day and of to-morrow. May they prove themselves equal to the great opportunity which the justifiable revolt of Labour has now afforded them.

Note Appearing in the Original Work
*See Rev. H. V. Mills' *Poverty and the State.*